SHADES *of* SHADE

DEVIKA V. WATKINS

Brilliant Books Literary
137 Forest Park Lane Thomasville
North Carolina 27360 USA

Thanks to You

Thank you to my family and friends
Thanks to all my colleagues and friends around this spherical bend
Thanks to Ms. Mosses, my English literature teacher, who made me
believe I can create my world with words from school
Her acceptance and belief in me eased my feelings of being filthy, inferior, filthy and poor

Thanks to the people whom I discovered and surround
Thanks for your inspiration and stories that astound

Thanks to my husband, so damn gorgeous, loving, and kind
Thanks to him for helping me to control this bipolar mind
Thanks to my beautiful little daughter, so beautiful, social, pure, and kind
She made me believe in angels, fairies, goodness, and humankind

Thanks to these willing artists from around the world
Thanks to them for believing, envisioning, and creating my
poems into their unique artistic colorful swirls
Thanks again, my willing artists, for all your labors and pain
You've invested time, put aside your lives
To help me create and leave a grain

Thank you readers, for giving me a chance
I am trusting that I am worthy for you to take a second glance.

Table of Contents

Fog

Illustrated by Sofia Moustahfid

Fog

Mist and fog seem to be the theme for every day
She sits at the window wondering what day is today
Her faded beauty is as prominent as her shock of silvery grays
Reality seems to be kept at bay

Beside her stands a dressing table laden with glittering oversize jewels
All of which are acquired by exotic and worldly travels
A little blue sparkle of gemstone in the light
Makes her smile with a spark of delight

She saw herself twenty-three and free
Dark-brown hair flowing in the breeze
At the vendor's table, the blue spark caught her eyes
And she moved as if mesmerized
She reached to pick it up with her graceful jeweled hand
As the jewel was swiftly snatched by a large hand that was very tanned
Eyes raised, she locked his gaze
As he held up the blue jewel next to his smiling dimpled face
Her memory halted, just as it had started
Blocking out the rest of that day

She shook her head, as if to clear this misty haze
But nothing seems to free her from this opaque glaze
When she opened her mouth to reveal her long-lost tale
The words froze on her lips
As fog prevailed

Annoyance, anger, and anxiety stirred her being
Her frustrations seemed to be the only real thing
She bolted up and walked out the door
Not looking back at her wealthy galore
Hoping to break this foggy state
She headed to the park and the fountain by the gate

In the sun, she captured large breaths of fresh, fragrant grassy air
And enjoyed all of life's natural fare
Water cascaded, spraying mists on her face
And she saw the fountain in Marrakech
She strolled, and she smiled and sat for a while
Closing her very tired eyes

She awakes with a start
The day has turned dark
She is sitting in St. Stephen's Green Park
What is she doing here, only God knows
She gets up to return home, not wanting to be alone
Her body moves on through the darkness and haze
While her mind plays, and replays, "Is this the way?".

Long-Distance Love   Illustrated by Tania Canteli

Long-Distance Love

Send me a message
Or call me on the telephone
This is a burden my heart has borne
This distance of water, the difference of time
Cannot change my intense state of mind

In my loneliness, I relive our shared bliss
The memories help my gloom to blow away
I listen to our songs
They make me reminisce
I long for your embrace
I long for your kiss
But all I have to go on
Is your image in the mist

The nightingale has sang its song
The sparrow was here
And now it's gone
The new moon is glowing in the dark
The stars are looking for a reason to spark

Ring, ring, ring
It's almost weekend
It's the telephone
And I feel like leaping
My heart's racing really fast
Racing past Venus, Earth, Jupiter, and Mars

Hello sweetheart
Hello darling
Did you miss me?
Are you coming this weekend?
I am waiting
Daydreaming, hoping, and anticipating

Hello my love
I miss you so much
Why are you shedding tears like rain?
Don't you know you're my sparkling champagne?

Ann

Illustrated by Aliaksandra Kavalenka

Ann

Born in a wealthy family
In a household where they did not live happily
Little Ann was considered a calamity
Her mother decided to take precautions
Because Dad did not want another mouth to feed
Thus leaving Ann to face an orphaned life and tragedy

With her little dour face, donated dress, and slate
Little Ann was left to face her fate
Five brothers and four sisters, all with families or lives of their own
Little Ann was headed to a destination unknown

The house she lived in changed
When her sister took another's name
She was moved to a beautiful wooden house facing the sea
Where calm waters and breezy trees offered her serenity
After school, she would do all her chores
She swept and scrubbed
Until little hands were raw with blood
For all little Ann wanted was to be loved and hugged

Three children were born in the house Little Ann called home
That was when she knew this house was never her own
She became cook, cleaner, babysitter
She became mom, dad, and storyteller
They loved her, she knew
She was their critical glue
She watched her sister become battered and bruised
She was the only shield to protect the younger three from being abused

Ann was taken abroad without consent of her own
She lived with a brother and his wife
Who did not want Ann in their lives
When brother was gone to work one day
Sister-in-law took Ann on a trip on the subway
Intending for it to be a journey, one-way
Knowing Ann didn't know this foreign country or her way

In panic and dismay, heart laden with pain
Ann discovers one token to the train
She returned in the cold and in the rain
To face a life of disdain

Ann was reported, locked up, and tried
She was deported back to the land from whence she came
Now back in the sunshine and the rain
Ann felt as if kept in chains

She wanted more than this life of being denied
She wanted love and care and pride
She wanted most to be his special bride
But again, her love was denied

The neighbors' son loved her, he proclaimed
This which later brought Ann a name of shame
For she was pregnant with only herself and hard circumstances to blame
They married after the baby was born
While facing his family's scorn
She had a home, a life, and was someone's wife
But the price to pay, she was living another's life

Three kids grown
Again, Ann mourns
For her eldest son died alone
Reasons unknown

Once again tragedy and death
Uprooted Ann from her family life and the love she had bred
Leaving her with a heart that bled
Wandering again in the sunshine and the rain
Ann's life is bound by chains of pain.

Games

Illustrated by Morris Callegari

Games

Man watch dem women when they come out to play
Lips, tips, and hair in place
Dem dress in their best, looking indiscreet
Strutting their stuff to be noticed in the street

Dem a tease, nah willing to please
They would get you hard
They would drive you mad
'Cause dem a tease, nah willing to please
They would treat you bad
And leave you sad

In the club, dem change dem tune
Face light up, bright like the moon
Inviting every man to take she hand
So she can dance to the band
Oh geez, oh man
Look how she ah get on

She love the music
She ah throw up her hand
She love the rhythm
She ah wine up on de man

Watch she how she ah dance with grace
Then she start to move she waist
Her eyes flashing with mischief in her eyes
Her lips curl into that flirtatious smile

You dance all night, holding her tight
Then you kiss her on the floor
Oh geez, you feel your heart soar
Then daylight break
The gal disappear without a trace
No digits, no name
Yuh learn her game.

Beautiful Woman   Illustrated by Sofia Moustahfid

Beautiful Woman

Woman walks into the room
Not loud but quite proud
Everyone notices her face
Because of her beauty and grace
Everyone thinks they know what they see
But no one knows, only friends and me
Her dark hair's short and tight
Dimples enhanced by light
But this lass, although carefree and free
Has battled many stormy seas

Her high-pitched voice is very smooth
This tool with which she uses to soothe
She listens and nods and comforts when she can
Her advice and opinion are never secondhand
Though her stance is unbiased
She let it be known she's not pious
She's learned to comfort chaos and pain
But yet never with disdain

This petite being is a giant's treat
This fragile one cannot be beat
Her temper's cool
Her name probably means pure
Of this, I'm really damn sure
Not because she's a saint portrayed
But is a fighting soul that cannot be swayed

Thank you lady, who takes flight
Thank you for being such a delight
Claim your day
I know you'll not be fazed
Claim the night with wondrous sights

Share your journeys beyond wide seas
And know that we recognize energies
Thank you lady, for sharing your glare
Thank you lady, beyond compare

While we are here, we only have love to share
Your message is homebound
We will choose whom we surround
Our comet that shines so bright
You're the spark that continues to share your light

Thank you lady, thank you girl
I'm really thankful to have met you in this world.

Only Four   Illustrated by Victoria Mace

Only Four

I'm only four, I don't know much more
All I know is Daddy's home
Without him, I'd be all alone
He said Mama was here, but now she's gone
Gone from here to the great beyond

I want my mom
I promise to do all my chores until they're done
I want my mom
To pick me up when I fall down

I see her face
I remember her smiles
I swear, she really looked like the queen of the Nile
I love my dad, but he's just so sad
He talks of Mama and the love they had

Mama, I promise to be good through and through
If that's what it'll take to get a hug from you
I remember your love
I remember your touch
I still remember your smell that I loved so much

Now I'm five, and Papa has finally showed me where Mama lay
She lays with the flowers
A part of nature
Just like the birds and the bees
She lays on the moors
Under the sunshine and the trees

I know now Mama's never coming back from beyond
I know now, especially since Daddy's wedding is on

I promise Mama, to be good to my mama who's new
But I promise Mama, I'll never stop loving you.

Blow   Illustrated by Amanda Narain

Blow

Love is supposed to be kind
It's supposed to make you feel free
Love is supposed to give strength
It's supposed to be honesty
But what about those who are not fortunate to experience this ideology?

She started out shy and pure
Got married to a man from the military school
Fell in love, then two kids were born
Thus creating a complete home

They worked and built
Their circle of love fulfilled
One day after work, she returned home
To find her husband gone and kids alone
She waited and prayed
Hoping he had not strayed
But all this hoping was just in vain
He returned home with a streetwalker in tow
Using drinks and drugs and things that blow

She begged and she pleaded
But came up defeated
For this family man's heart was depleted
Distraught and hurt, she threatened family court
He just laughed in her face
Knowing she couldn't live on only child support

Life became unbearable
With lack of respect and behavior that was terrible
But because she was mother of two
She put up, shut up, and lived as part of this zoo

Broken heart, now numb from pain
She met a man who promised to shelter her from the rain
They loved and they played
It was a love mismatched from the minute it was made

Time went by
Husband bore news of the cancerous kind
All of a sudden, he wanted her there
Her support, her love, and his burdens to share
Despite her hate
She felt sorrow for his state
And stood by him, waiting for his maker to deliberate

He prayed to God and mourned his loss of lust
He prayed that she would take him back
Blaming God for being unjust
During this fiasco
Her lover proved himself shallow
He cheated on her
An event which was destined to follow

Together again
Both bruised and shamed
He's playing family man
She's looking for the next best game.

Nyla

Illustrated by Aliaksandra Kavalenka

Nyla

Sparkling eyes gleam
In a face that reflects a polished sheen
Exterior appearances created with precision
Not leaving anything for interpretation
This created facade is as thin as a fairy's veil
Yet not exposing her interior tale

Day, months, years go by
And as the decades evolve
She lives her life with a stern resolve
To be good and kind and free
Not creating enmity

But deep within, emotions churn
Causing her soul to burn
Everything she worked so hard to achieve
Feels like strangled liberty
For being trapped by childhood pain
Feels like just cause to go insane

Mama was there, frozen or numb
To this day, Nyla does not know which one
When stepfather chose to cash in on Nyla's unearned income
He said women were only good for one thing
To take care of a man and be his plaything
Through childhood, she did not know what he meant
These words now is the cause of her torment
His vile illegal acts now leave her feeling broken and bent
Now all she wants is to take shelter and vent
Hoping to overcome the trauma she underwent

Men come and go
Whether it's for real or show
I don't think she really knows
Because fighting to survive is her ultimate goal
Who really cares about her, her hell or her toll?

Cycle of Life   Illustrated by Tania Canteli

Cycle of Life

The innocence of their stare
The wonder of the sun's glare
Everything's so fresh and new
Even the early morning dew

The fascination in their eyes
Gives them a look, as if hypnotized
The burning hunger for more in life
That even the passing years cannot derive

With the passing of the growing years
They develop very distinguished airs
Some becoming very fortunate heirs
And can acquire anything, anytime, anywhere
They live in splendor and lavish glamour
Yet their eyes tell of their broken demeanor

Others, not becoming very prosperous with the years
Survive in life, burdened by cares and fears
They long for needs to be relieved
And long dreamed desires to be acquired
Yet through all the misery and pain
They find means to stay out of the rain

To compare the two would truly relate this zoo
The fortune and the unfortunate
Would all have touching stories to relay
Some have stories of riches and fame
Others battling the devil's game
But side by side they look like one
Both holding stares from far beyond

They yearn for youth and go searching for the truth
Some investing the rest of their lives
To replace that youthful sparkle in their eyes
And just when they thought the walls are closing in
True light comes shining forth from within

They live their lives
Whether rich or poor
And take long walks in the heat and in the cool

They left their mark, whether blunt or sharp
Each had a spark
That made them put up until they depart
Each leaving something for another to end or start.

De Good Woman   Illustrated by Kabria Smith

De Good Woman

He wanted a good woman
A woman with no shame
A religious woman, a woman with no name

This preacher man begotten her hand
And together they were supposed to become one
Well, this man, a fool at heart
Took his prize, ready to start
Then passion took root and blossomed its fruits
De good woman turned around and got herself a name
A name that brought this town to shame

She wanted fame, and fame got her a name
A name that shamed a pimp at his game
She bragged and she boasted
She lied and was loathed
But she, the woman, was queen in reign

She de woman, de good good woman
Showed this fool who's best at this game
When a man set out to choose
He should select the heart that is true
'Cause de woman, de good good woman
Will take your heart and rip it right through

She wanted fame, that fame gave her a name with shame
Oh, how this man wished he had brains
He lost his house, a brand-new BMW
Half his earnings
Oh god, how he wished he knew

He got the woman
The chaos and the pain
All this drove the fool insane.

Jewel of the Nile   Illustrated by Amanda Narain

Jewel of the Nile

The glamour of pearls, the dazzle of diamonds
The fire of rubies, that's my jewel
The jewel of my life
That emerged from the Nile
For through the darkness, she brought forth the light

I basked in her light and soaked up the warmth
Just to discover that old feeling of love
This spark of life, this fiery being
Slipped in my life and disappeared into the night
Now I'm back to earth and looking for my comet's light

She left her mark like footprints engraved in stone
Now I'm seeking this goddess for my throne
Help me find my shining jewel
This feeling neither heaven nor hell could dispel

Come, my lady, because you're my light
You're the reason I put up this fight
Hear my pleas, understand my plight
Pay attention 'cause I'm yours
And I won't give up until this dream is ours

Come back baby, because you're my light
You're my shining jewel of the Nile.

Shade of Shades   Illustrated by Julie De Abreu

Shade of Shades

Isn't it amazing we like and dislike based on shade?
Isn't this a pure and simple disgrace?
We look at one another in our face, and all we see is shade of shades
In our own race, there exist worlds that we cannot seem to change
He's too dark, she's black
Light-skinned, jet-black
Blackie, brownie
Do you know how these learned labels impact?
You know I'm stating fact

They leave gaping wounds that bleed
They make one weary and take heed
Just because you see color and not within
Treating it and me as a deadly sin

We should be one people, one nation
And we're supposed to be one family
Instead, we are our own worst enemy
Destroying one another's own destiny
Pointing fingers, calling each other ugly
Why this hate?
It's the strongest weapon to segregate
What can we do to change this embedded template?

When will we realize that our predators chose to divide and conquer
That they wanted to be superior
Thus making us inferior by pointing out our obvious exterior?

Does it make you better?
Do you feel whole?
When will we dig ourselves out of this vicious wormhole?
Why do we choose to follow the enemy's path?
When will we face facts?
Color is just skin-deep
It has nothing to do with our humanity

We all have burdens to bear
Why not treat one another fair?
We all have gifts to share
Take the time to recognize one another's flair
Give each other an equal stand
And let's carve our own path, hand in hand.

Variety of Life

Illustrated by Aliaksandra Kavalenka

Variety of Life

Variety is the spice of life
But variety can all turn into vice
She's dating this trio
Hoping they'll give her a direction to follow

Number 1 is involved in his own world
He thinks everything is about him, not her
He wants everything in sight
Yet he behaves quite uptight
She's thinking about letting him slip
Just because he's not ready to commit

Number 2 is in love with himself
I wouldn't be surprised if he left in the shelf
He brags and boasts
And it's never on a very good note
If he's not ready to take heed
She'll have to treat him like tumbleweed

Number 3 gives her the blues
He's in love with her
And is professing he'll love her forever
She's not ready for him quite yet
All she sees him as, is her security net

I hope she sorts out her confusion
And discovers true love and passion
This is all she wants in life
To build a future, a home, and be a good wife

I hope she keeps her options open
Just not to have to deal with a future burden
Don't put all your eggs in the same basket
Look around, inquire, and make time to invest
Only then you can expect that true, everlasting marital request.

Lesbian Woman

Illustrated by Aliaksandra Kavalenka

Lesbian Woman

Hello girl, hello you
Look at me, I'm talking to you
You want a man like me to show you who's who
Why are you ignoring me, do you think you know what to do?
I can change you with my six inches of fun
I'll make you a real, proper woman

Why you walk around like a man of all seasons?
Who do you think you are?
I'll give you purpose and reasons
I'll give you an unforgettable ride
Maybe then you can develop some pride
Stop with all your mannish side

What can a woman give you?
Why don't you get a clue?
Your behavior is quite unnatural
Wanting a woman is very abnormal
Eve did not find Eve
It was Adam who planted his seed

Wait, stop, someone help me, please . . .
Can't anyone see, I'm just me?
What did I do to deserve this tide?
Who do you think you are, trying to make me hide?

This is how I was born
I do not deserve this hatred and scorn
I'm your mom, your sister, your neighbor, who knows?
These are all mortal blows
Live my life, walk in my shoes
Then tell me, what you will choose?

I'm a woman
Small, big, short, tall
Do you think you can stifle us all?
Stop bullying me every day
Open your eyes, I was born this way

I cannot change from black to white
I cannot turn day into night
I cannot stop the current of deep blue seas
I cannot put leaves back on dead trees
I cannot change death to life
Why do you think my way of life
Is premeditated strife?

We all possess a soul
We all have different roles
Appreciate the difference
Inform your ignorance
Stem this tide of intolerance

Breathe new air
In this world we share
Plant new deeds
Evolve from pestering weeds
Into self-supporting, life-giving, magnificent trees.

Spice of Life　　　　　　　　　Illustrated by Amanda Narain

Spice of Life

She looked at him, he looked back
Then from within smiles came forth
This human heart was not built for cold
Share the love, feel it soar

It may cause pleasure, it may cause pain
Either way, live your life
Don't just sacrifice

The sky's the limit, the valleys are deep
Keep this heart young and free
Preserve youth, it's the key to unlock sensuality

She touched his hair, he kissed her lips
This started a fairy tale of bliss
Flowers blossom, fruits are borne
Plant the seed, watch it grow
Create the fantasy, provide the illusion
Present the stage for temptation

They shared bodies beyond space and time
This started Cupid's theme and rhyme
"Will you be my Valentine?"

Red and white, yellow and black
These are shades of spices in the pack
Share the flavors, experience the zest
This is the aroma of life at its best.

Little Soldier   Illustrated by Baba Mustapha

Little Soldier

Speech is slurred
Vision's blurred
Her facade is dissipating
With friends coming and leaving
Family knows her pain, yet she struggles to get out of the rain

Memories unfold
Truths are untold of misery, chaos, and pain
Thus transforming this gentle human to mush
And brain without brains

Slap then scream
She races to war
Father's standing, Mother's on the floor
Trembling with bone-chilling fear, this soldier's time is here

Little hands uplift to create peace and stop the blows
Little body tries to block out only God knows
Mamma's crying
Father's flogging
Children shivering
While this little soldier's brave swollen face displays eyes that are bleeding

One cry and yelp
While the other tries to find help
Just to be told, "Some women like that"
This is worse than being kicked and slapped

Little soldier stands up straight and short
Little soldier tries to block out hurt
Sacrifice is the aim of the day
Survive is the only way
This little person has been pushed beyond her years
Hiding fears and holding back a flood of tears

Little soldier beauty's faded and gone
Leaving behind this tired grown sun
Wobbly, drunken smiles
That does not quite reach her eyes
This soldier is fighting battles for miles

Share your love
Listen to her thoughts
For only then change can spark
Battles have been fought
Battles are here
Battles just does not seem to disappear
Senses gets numb
This soldier is done
Again, every single drop is gone

Bottle rolls away
Soldier floats away
Please help her before her time is nigh.

Winners and Losers   Illustrated by Morris Callegari

Winners and Losers

Snake eyes, deuce is wild
Slot machines beeping
Winners going wild

Lights flashing
Go-go girls dancing
Music blasting
Performers competing
Throw the dice, pull your card
Close your eyes and pray to God

Winners realize and shout with glee
Losers pull out of the crowd very discreetly
This kind of gambling is for real
Because you can get hooked like a fish at the end of a reel

Watch the pack, players, and your card
Don't slack off 'cause you might go mad
Keep your face straight and hard
Don't twitch, wink, and give away your facade
Calculate the game, make your aim
Throw the dice and win the game

Winning is sweet
Losers turn blue
The trouble is it's me against you
Play the game fierce and hard
Then you can turn around and make truce with your pal.

Ladies-in-Waiting

Illustrated by Aliaksandra Kavalenka

Ladies-in-Waiting

She paced the floor back and forth
Counting seconds, minutes, and hoping he would call on the telephone
Her heart was quaking with a turmoil of emotions
Just to hear from him with anticipation
Robbie, thinking she was going nowhere
Pranced around like he just didn't care

His best friend contacted her a few hours later, saying Robbie would be right over
Knowing she was kept in waiting
They started talking, giggling, and laughing

Then Robbie's best friend invited her out
He showed her the east, the west, the north, and the south
Now that she was out and did not feel very devout
She turned around and kissed Robbie's best friend on the mouth

Men, don't keep your ladies waiting
They're not just your simple plaything
Ladies-in-waiting, ladies-in-waiting
Are there just for the right timing

Now Robbie's heart is breaking
He'll be in the wedding
When the leaves are shedding
He is the best man in the wedding
To witness the marriage of his best friend to his darling.

Narkis   Illustrated by Wojciech Dudzinski

Narkis

When I think of her, red and pink comes to mind
Reminding me of Mother Time
Wild and free, spirit full of glee
Ancestry from the Black Sea
What a treat it is to be around this gypsy-minded individual
Personality and humor are positively sinful

Do not let this *malka yafa*'s exterior fool you
She has knowledge and experience that can school
She was mom, sister, and role model to two younger brothers
For life was not easy for their mother
Through trial and error
Life became clearer
They each developed their own distinguished personalities
With their own lives and families

Now she is mother to three
Their home is happy and free
For this is what she always aspired to be
Earthy, colorful, bohemian, and eclectic
Her surroundings are properly shabby chic

Exterior of a proper belle
Her heart is as delicate as an ostrich shell
She is a giver, she is a sharer
She is a teacher, she is a preacher
Celebrating life now comes easier with her ingenuity
In her everyday life, she seizes every opportunity

Sometimes in moments of doubts and questions
Arise opportunities for unearthed directions
But even in moments of weakness and need
She draws experience from her family tree
Let's nurture this savvy flower
For within beauty and color, there is power.

Rage   Illustrated by Amanda Narain

Rage

Rage, rage, rage, man with rage
Going through life, appearances of a sage
He beat the kids and slapped their face
Creating looks of turmoil and disgrace
They harbored feelings of hate and anger
Waiting when the time was right, to get away from this monster

He beat the wife and marked her face
Punching, kicking, and slapping
And if her face still held grace
This coward kept on with his tirade
When she fell and eyes rolled back
Then he stepped back and face went slack
He left the house looking dapper and feeling like a king in reign
Not realizing his behavior was quite insane

Clueless girl who didn't know danger and pain, left her house
All part of his preplanned game
He treated her like a queen
Manners and chivalry flowing like a well-oiled machine
Bubbles erupting, emotions connecting, they drank, dined, and chatted
While this man's hopes took flight like a bat
After dinner, he kissed her, and her innocent heart soared
After which he opened the car door
His car glided to his destination, with images of anticipation

As the evening wore on, she said she was unsure
Realizing she needed to make a path for the door
Then rage took aim, this man did not like to feel lame
So he turned around and whacked her, just as she was saying his name
The shock and fear, head spinning like a wheel
Made her realize that her danger was real
She started to run, then he pulled out a gun
And told her to shut up, otherwise she was done

Rage, rage, rage, this man closed his cage
And injured the innocent, battered, and disgraced
She returned home feeling vile and torn
That was when the innocent mother's anger was born

Mom picked up the knife and left right away
Showed up at his house with not a word to say
He opened the door, not remembering anymore
When the mother's knife sliced with galore
Rage, rage, rage spewed on the floor and left this man
No longer the devil's spore

Rage, rage, rage, you better turn a new page.

Black Sheep   Illustrated by Tania Canteli

Black Sheep

Please don't be unkind
Your words are harsh and leave scars in my mind
But even though some of your words are true
It does no good to make me sad and unsure
You rant and rave and point fingers in my face
All of which for me create shame and disgrace

You said I've always been the black sheep
According to you, I do not choose with whom and where I sleep
Maybe you should walk in my shoes and live my life
Only then you can realize
That reality is just a trigger away
A fact I've had to deal with from day to day

You disagree with the things I do and say
Not respecting I have my own way
The love and hate you feel
Is quite unnatural, leaving me a raw deal

I wish you'd open your eyes and realize
That life for some of us is like desert lands haunted by needs and wants
This fact of life, although well-known
Is looked upon with hatred and scorn

I see no shades and choose not to segregate by color or race
My love is my way of life that's unprejudiced
Your opposite opinion that cannot be dismissed
I'm trying to live based on the way I feel
But society has created barriers of steel

I may have broken rules and created taboo
But my life is about me and my heart that is trying to stay true

I am me and cannot be what you want me to be
I am me and refuse to bend the knee
I make no apologies for seeing beyond my years
I make no apologies for wanting to be free.

Quiet Man   Illustrated by Julie De Abreu

Quiet Man

Quiet man, quiet man
Your time has come
Quiet man, quiet man
You're in the sun
Hold your head up high and proud
Raise your stammering voice, way up loud

So far, you've stayed in shadows
Stepping back when life bellowed
Chapters start, stories end
All of which you pretend
That this life is too big for you
A place where dreams cannot come true

Quiet man, quiet man
Your knowledge and drive
Have made you deal with sacrifice, heartache, and strife
Thus building character to strengthen your soul
To balance life and ultimate goals

Look again, you can fight this bashful stain
Because you're now a man with a name
Established, fine, and beyond compare
Stop bowing your head, and hold their stares

Quiet man, quiet man
Stop procrastinate
And focus your sights to the lady waiting at your gate
She's really quite near, don't make her wait
This is one chance, you cannot be late
You've journeyed marathon miles
Stepping out, no longer shy, but bold
For finally you can see the whole

Quiet man, quiet man
Quiet no more
Quiet man, quiet man
You've finally unlocked life's galore.

Struggles   Illustrated by Corlette Douglas

Struggles

"As I walk in the valley of shadow of death, I shall fear no evil"
Nice try, but not the truth
I would have liked not to fear evil
Yet evil found me, it found us
They found our color and was threatened by us

They were amazed by our stance or strengths and our ways
They were amazed by our determination, and our intelligence
Despite the barriers and traps set up
We were not fazed
Yes, they were amazed

Evil came in many, not just one face
In our case
It came in the minds and deeds of the pale face
We are not pale
We are not small
We are not picky
And we do not covet another man who has it all

However, we are trusting
Ready to make amends
Working around corners and bends
Just to let the natural and unnatural blend
Yes, we are trusting

We are scattered like spores because there were doubts among few
Thus not creating a strong enough glue

I was captured, I was chained
I was beaten until I was numb from pain
I was bought, I was sold
I was enslaved
I was worked, I was raped
All this to prevent escape

I was suffocated, I was drowned
I was tortured, I was hung
To make me walk with my head held down
Yes, all this was done

Our inventions and input were not accredited
Yet our structures and kingdoms were coveted
Thus, they tried to wipe out our features and spark
Creating their own corrupted monarch
Our sacred beliefs caused us mockery and death
For they imitated shrouded white figures
Flaming crosses, guns, and swords with a sheath
The threat is the glare of illumination from our minds
The structure and built of our kind

I relay misdeeds, not to create hate and enmity
But to make aware our history
To remind us of our equality
To spread love and integrity
To make better a place for humanity

We have love, we care
Let's create a better world for the children we bear
For only through love and peace
We can prevent the repeat of history

Open your eyes, create a path
Have yourself a baptismal bath
And emerge clean and pure
Even though your footsteps might be unsure
Remind yourself that every breath, every thought, and every action might create an equal reaction
Lead by example, without hidden agendas
Knowing when we depart
We have led a path that giants might impart.

Roxanne   Illustrated by Patricia Tan

Roxanne

Roxanne, what kind of day is it going to be today?
Will it be lived their or your way?
You've fixed your smile in place
Even though you face distaste
This life without freedom and challenges presented by the almighty kingdom
Leaves you raw and fearsome

Wanting to be you, Roxanne
Has caused you labels and names
People thinking this is some kinda game
Wanting to be you is pure taboo
Regardless of your clothes, your style, or your shoes
Beautiful Roxanne, what will you do?
This everyday life is killing you
Going through life
People treat you like you're a freak
I guess when it comes to you and your kind
You're shrouded in mystique

You brace yourself and clench your teeth
For they're too narrow-minded to see how you're unique
As a child, I waited for your smiles
For I thought you had the most beautiful eyes
The kindness you showed fell on deaf ears
Just because of their ignorant fears
You were labeled "antiman"
No one seemed to recognize that you are human
They threw rocks and stones
And didn't care if you were shredded to your bare bones

Beautiful Roxanne, I still remember you
You had to flee family, town, and home
Even though this was where you were born
Born a man, you are, Roxanne
For you are trapped in a "his" body, this life, this zoo
Trying to prove you're a woman and you're somebody too
Beautiful Roxanne, I wonder where you roam
I most certainly hope you've found somewhere to call home.

Picture-Perfect   Illustrated by Sofia Moustahfid

Picture-Perfect

Picture taken, picture-perfect
Pictures to have year after year
Pictures that will never disappear

She sets moods and creates interludes
Shooting picture-perfect settings
Can become quite breathtaking
She gets lost and becomes a romantic
As scenes develop and become dramatic

She travels over rivers and wide seas
To find that special serenity on the breeze
She locates buildings and picks out trees
All to be part of life's many scenes

She seeks nothingness to discover more
To display and discover life's galore
Through the lens, she takes note of corners and bends
And, in her mind's eye, makes amends
Making sure natural and created blends
Giving everything needed and setting trends

Her creation takes on a life on its own
That nags and tugs at the soul
Making you want more

The lights explode, capturing the episode
And everything prepared are no longer codes
In the heat and in the cold
She sweats and shivers
But the scene's never left alone
Not until it's all together and airborne

Her creation and devotion will soon be known
Even if she's here, gone or alone
The last scene shot
She picks up her sack
And heads through the crowd
Never turning back

She's with her friend
A friend to the end
That piece of glass
That will make her forever last.

Family Man   Illustrated by Aliaksandra Kavalenka

Family Man

I live lies
I live fantasies
I wear disguises
And make myself available to please

I hang out in wild pubs and nightclubs
And toy around with sharks and dogs
Their games are rough, and lessons tough
But in all, I see diamonds in the rough

Their lives are colorful and diverse
And their pickup lines are well rehearsed
Looking for good game, happiness, or the perfect situation
Can make one quite disillusioned

They cross thresholds and create barriers
And become lovers and warriors
They all fight for the same dream
Even though their scars are deeper than treacherous streams

One by one, they drop out of the crowd
Holding their heads up high and proud
They finally found their destined dame
To carry on the family name

Living perfect TV lives
They work religiously from nine to five
They are now molded breadwinners
No longer everyday calculating sinners

Heads of their households
And making up very strict, unbreakable rules
They're sending their children to the best colleges and schools

They create customs and traditions
Trying anything to preserve their family as one
And building a strong generation.

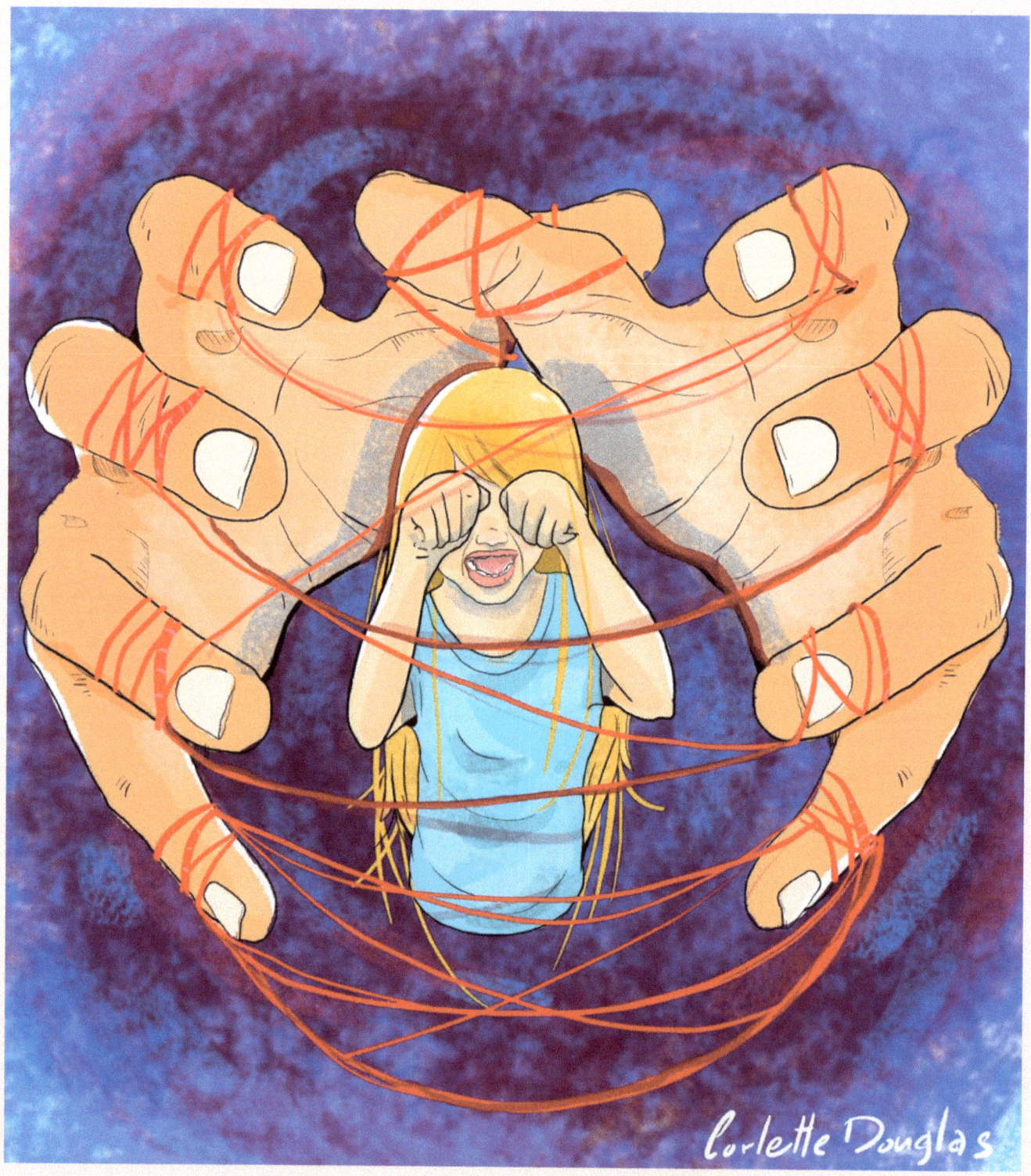

Silent, Loud Little Cries   Illustrated by Corlette Douglas

Silent, Loud Little Cries

"Leave me alone, I don't want to go."
"Why?"
"I don't know."
Stop this. Behave. Don't make me late
You're always acting up, why this hate?
Big blue eyes
Staring up at the skies
Big blue eyes that tell no lies.
Mama is busy, Dad too
Both working hard to provide shelter and food

"Auntie's there, she'll take care of you."
That was what she thinks, if only she knew
No one to hear, no one to care
She was frightened to death of the lady with the blond hair

Spanked, pushed, and shoved
Slapped with a glove
"Help me, Michael, only you know love."
"No talking to him, no playing
Now stay in this room,
I don't care if you're afraid of the gloom."

"Come get me, Mama, I'm wet and cold
She doesn't care, she said I was bold
Where are you, why don't you hear?
Will no one listen to my despair?"

Uncle showed up from work at five.
He finally extracted me from this beehive
He understood I was a child of only three
His manner kind, and he treated me gently
I loved him, he was my "cookie people"
He was my strength, my shining steeple

"The inconvenience of it all
Why is she so disruptive to us all?
Sorry Clare, I know we're friends
Sorry about my child and her bad bends."

"My name is Kate, I know it's a bit late
Only as an adult, someone finally listened and told my story behind my hate."

Glitz, Fame, and Power

Illustrated by Aliaksandra Kavalenka

Glitz, Fame, and Power

Glitz, fame, and power are the luxuries we all desire
Some work hard
Some work smart
And some just live off another

Woman nah want a man who have nothing to do
Dem want a man with promising value
Man nah want woman that a behave like dem lame
Dem want a woman with a preplanned game

So for all the diamond seekers
Look harder and deeper
Dem seh the world is wide and the sky go higher
So develop a reach like a rubber

Woman, put yuh package together
Stay away from appearances that will bore
Create a body men want more
And develop a career that will make you soar

Man, get yuh act together
Take a woman that is faithful
Nah bother with the gal that is glamorous and ungrateful

Get yuh glitz, fame, and power
That yuh all desire
Work harder, smarter
And nah bother leach off another.

Wings of Love   Illustrated by Amanda Narain

Wings of Love

Your heart aches
And the pain you feel seems impossible to relate
The loss, the horror, the helplessness of all
Is a crushing blow to your world
You feel regret and blame,
As acute and hot as a searing flame
Burning your senses
With the image that is charred into your brain

You wish you can change the decision you made
You wish you can take back everything of that day
You heard my cry, then saw me lifted to the sky
Frozen with horror and fear
You could not believe your eyes
You cringed to think what became of me
This, your human senses could not envision my end to be

My mother, my sister, my friend, my caregiver
What wonderful words for protector
You gave me a safe home
You gave me eighteen years which I would not have had on my own
You gave me a world which we shared
You gave me Love beyond compare
You gave your days, your nights, your thoughts, your soul
You forgot that every bond has its toll

This joining of worlds, you and me
Is impossible in nature, as binding sky to sea
Yet we're tied, you heart and mine
This which will forever be Divine
I'm of the heavens, you're of earth
But we'll both end up as part of this cyclical dirt

The world I come from is wild and free
Where the cycle of life spins without missing a beat
Though beautiful, and colorful, and bountiful in its state
It's also brutal and unprejudiced in every creature where instinct is used to deliberate

It was an honor to be gifted with my time spent with you
But what an honor to return to my maker in a manner that's true
In the skies where I belong
Higher and higher, my taker took me
Back to my maker, fulfilling my destiny
My time is done
Please let me go back to my universe and beyond.
Dry your tears and celebrate my years
Heal your heart for one day in the distance of space and time
We'll have no wings and hands, only eternal sunshine.

The Note   Illustrated by Aliaksandra Kavalenka

The Note

You took my breath away
When you gave me the note that day
You smiled when I questioned with my eyes
Your note said, "When a stranger meets a stranger"
I kept reading, not knowing my heart was in danger
Your words started to build a hunger
Which I know expressed all my desires

Oh my angel in disguise, I met you in the skies
You said I was placed in the heavens
You failed to see my temptations
This revelation had left me in a turmoil of emotions
Free me from this damnation

Each day when I awake
I'm tempted to call
But I'm afraid of what to say
You said you wanted to know the angel behind the beauty
Now because of you
My heart's behaving quite unruly

I would like to sit and talk with you
Just to find out if your words were true
And even though we're strangers through and through
Your note made us one, me and you
Whatever life has in store
Your words lifted me up and made me soar
You're my miracle in being
Your words for me are like reversing autumn to spring.

Thank You Mom   Illustrated by Sofia Moustahfid

Thank You Mom

Thank you Mom, for giving me life
Thank you for not choosing the knife
Though I'm not against this act in times of need
We should be wanted seeds and not created by vicious misdeeds

Thank you Mom, for keeping your grace and honor
And not being bent by another's temper
This journey you faced of love and hate
Was impossible for one to deliberate

Trapped by three and our many needs
You found a miraculous way to provide encouragingly
You taught and sang and baked
We especially loved your "red-flower" sponge cake

We painted paper with powder colors
Patiently you showed us how to make Chinese lanterns
And using crayons to trace window patterns
Through need and skill, we learned to build
Celebrating life, which we fulfilled

Life was heaven and hell on earth
All dependent on whether you were happy or hurt
For in all the natural sunshine and watery island beauty
Serenity was shattered when adults behaved unruly

Your screams and cries still affect our lives
For your battery and pain was recorded by our very young eyes
Sobbing and in pain, you comforted us
For terror and hate and love were shown
An emotional roller coaster taking off on its own

Thank you Mom, for taking flight
Knowing your life would be filled with sacrifice
You toiled in the heat and in the cool
To send us to prestigious schools
And even though I flopped and failed
Your unconditional love still prevailed

Thank you Mom, for your presence and duty
Thank you for providing a world of beauty.

Featured Artists

Sofia Moustahfid
Damascus, Maryland

Artist and illustrator

My name is Sofia, and I am a freelance illustrator with a passion for visual storytelling. I am primarily interested in the visual impact of texture and color and the emotional quality of flowing lines and shapes. I strive to create pieces that evoke a feeling of nostalgia, as well as include subtle surrealistic elements. I love working with a wide variety of mediums, though my favorites would have to be oil and watercolor. My work can be found at sofieannart.com.

Patricia Tan
Quezon City, Philippines

Digital artist

Patricia Tan is a young graphic designer and illustrator based in the Philippines. She draws fan arts of various video games, animations, and comics. She studies history and a couple of languages in her spare time. When she is not drawing or reading, she is usually found sleeping. Her site is at https://dreamsandabyss.artstation.com.

Victoria Mace
León, Nicaragua

Professional administrative services | Proofreading and editing

You are the wordsmith; I am the polishing cloth. When you've sketched out your project and it needs to shine, I can help. I take my business administrative skills and mix them with production practices from experience in the arts to ensure your writing works. Starting with your idea, using your words as the medium, we'll work together to sculpt just the right document. My work is available at vic.e.mace@gmail.com.

Baba Mustapha
Lagos, Nigeria

Creative digital illustrator and animator

I have been drawing for as long as I can remember, and this led me to be a digital illustrator and animator. I have over ten years of experience working on projects for the advertising industry, media companies, and small and medium enterprises in a vast variety of fields. Over the duration of time worked, I have acquired several skills and experiences in handling complex tasks and providing reliable solutions in illustrations, motion graphics, 2-D flash / 3-D animations, and graphic design. I am currently a freelancer doing what I love, creating the best visual solutions for businesses and brand image. My work can be found at https://kirkira.com/portfolio/.

Julie De Abreu
Funchal, Portugal

Julie De Abreu is a Venezuelan artist currently based in Portugal. She started her illustration career in her homeland, but due to the difficult situation there, she had to leave before finishing it. Julie expresses herself with images and believes in the power they have to speak. Her website is https://juliedeabreu.com/

Kabria Smith
Maine

Kabra Smith is a Maine native and adopted New Yorker who expresses herself best through art and poetry, especially when speaking up is difficult. When she was a kid, she read Debbie Allen's beautifully illustrated Dancing in the Wings, a story about a young girl of color chasing her dreams against the odds. Years later, after a very difficult childhood and a rough start to adulthood, she has become that lead character in the story. She's become a woman pursuing her passions in spite of people's opinions or the past, often expressing feelings or themes associated with her hardships to help or connect with others. She enjoys drawing and painting in charcoal, acrylic, watercolors, oils, and gouache. She is constantly evolving and loves trying different mediums, never running short of ideas. Her work can be found on www.artbykabria.com.

Tania Canteli
Spain

Tania Canteli is a contemporary painter working primarily in multilayered abstracts of acrylics on canvas. Born in northern Spain where she lived until her early twenties, she exhibited a fascination for modern art from an early age. During the college years, she traveled throughout Europe and lived in Spain and the United Kingdom, moving later on to New York City to pursue studies and a career as a fashion designer. The color palette and dominant water theme are deeply rooted in her experience growing up in the north coast of Spain, a place infamous for its inclement weather, deep forests on intimidating mountains, rough coastline, and moody Atlantic waters. Her site is at www.taniacanteli.com.

Aliaksandra Kavalenka
Belarus

I come from the beautiful country of Belarus, which is right in the middle of Europe. Growing up there made me love and appreciate nature, and I often refer to it in my art. I enjoy drawing and painting people as there is nothing more beautiful than the human body. Three years ago, I moved to New York, and this city has become my source of endless inspiration with its beautiful people, architecture, and special vibes. My website is IG: @thekavalenka.

Morris Callegari
Belize

Morris is a Belizean American illustrator and concept artist from Berkeley, California. Morris has goals of working in the film and video games industry and prides himself on making characters with diverse features to match the diverse cultures he's grown up with, moving numerous times throughout the Bay Area and traveling around the world. Projects with messages like this are important to him, and he plans to work on more diverse projects as he pushes forward in his career. His website is https://morriscallegari.com/.

Corlette Douglas
Brooklyn, New York

My name is Corlette Douglas, an African American freelance illustrator from Brooklyn, New York, and a graduate from the Fashion Institute of Technology. I've been doing a couple of children's books for a while now, but never have I been part of a process where I had to design the real struggles facing us today as a community. Whether we are black, white, Indian, or Asian, we have a lot of personal hardships we each have or had to overcome. I hope with these amazing poems that every person who reads them gains a little insight. My work can be found at corcorart.squarespace.com.

Amanda Narain
Toronto, Canada

Amanda Narain here, born and raised in Toronto, Canada. My style is very unique, very raw, and natural with a tribal influence. It is very much an extension of my soul. Although there are differences among my illustrations, my paintings, and my fashion art, they are still tied together by dot and line work. Detail is something huge for me; that is where I come alive and create the story for each piece. I believe in love. I believe in peace. Respect me enough to let my energy radiate around me. Believe in my energy—believe in my art. And you'll catch a glimpse of my soul shining. My work can be found at www.ArtBookOfAmanda.com.

About the Author

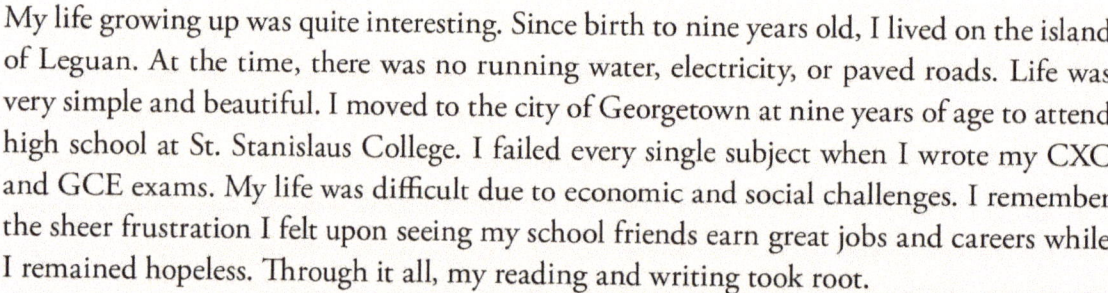

My name is Devika V. Watkins. I was born on a little island named Leguan, which is on the Essequibo River, Guyana. Guyana is quite unique in its state. It is a part of the South American continent and also part of the Caribbean. Guyana identifies with the culture of the Caribbean because Guyana was once colonized by the British.

My life growing up was quite interesting. Since birth to nine years old, I lived on the island of Leguan. At the time, there was no running water, electricity, or paved roads. Life was very simple and beautiful. I moved to the city of Georgetown at nine years of age to attend high school at St. Stanislaus College. I failed every single subject when I wrote my CXC and GCE exams. My life was difficult due to economic and social challenges. I remember the sheer frustration I felt upon seeing my school friends earn great jobs and careers while I remained hopeless. Through it all, my reading and writing took root.

I migrated with my family to the USA when I was eighteen years old. I attended LaGuardia Community College. I still remember the sheer hunger and joy I felt being given a second chance to go back to school. At the time, I was working and studying full-time. I have changed many jobs in my path to find myself. I am presently working in the airline industry as a Flight Attendant, and have been doing so since 1996. I have traveled vastly and have experienced many cultures and situations in my travels, which inspires me. While working full time with the airlines, I found my calling when I decided to pursue a degree in Interior Design at the Fashion Institute of Technology in New York City. Interior Design fulfilled the missing gap to my creative soul. I was inspired by the skills and vision of my professors and peers.

Because of my exposure to the world of Interior Design, I have been inspired to write and produce *Shades of Shade*, which is a coffee-table book containing my poetry and original works of art produced by twelve artists from different countries around the world.

My website address is devikavwatkins.com.